Real Live DRAGONS?

Written By: Anna DiGilio

All rights reserved. No part of this publication may be reproduced, distributed, or transmitted in any form or by any means, including photocopying, recording, or other electronic or mechanical methods, without the prior written permission of the publisher, except in the case of brief quotations embodied in critical reviews and certain other noncommercial uses permitted by copyright law.

For permission requests, write to the publisher:
Laprea Publishing
info@lapreapublishing.com

Website: www.GuidedReaders.com

ISBN: 978-1-64579-258-1

© 2019 Anna DiGilio

Photo Credits:
Cover, Title Page, 4: Adobe Stock; Antracit. 3: Depositphotos; Frenta. 5 (top), 6, 7 (bottom), 8 (top), 8 (bottom), 12 (top): Depositphotos; SURZet. 5 (bottom): Depositphotos; Tomgigabite. 7 (top): Depositphotos; Xtrekx. 7 (background), 10 (background): Depositphoto; Zajac. 9: Adobe Stock; Juulijs. 10 (top): Depositphotos; Krisrobin. 10 (bottom): Depositphotos; AirUbon. 11 (top): Adobe Stock; Uryadnikov Sergey. 11 (bottom): Adobe Stock; Nicole Lienemann. 12 (bottom left): Depositphotos; Oleksandr_UA. 12 (bottom right): Adobe Stock; Heathersheridan.

TABLE OF CONTENTS

Not the Dragon You Are
Thinking About!..Page 4

The Komodo Dragon..................................Page 6

The Bearded Dragon..................................Page 9

Glossary..Page 13

Not the Dragon You Are Thinking About!

When you picture a dragon, you may think of a scaly beast. It's breathing fire. It's fighting a knight. Perhaps it is in a storybook.

Dragons that fight knights and breathe fire are not real. Some people think these stories come from tales of dinosaurs or giant lizards.

Komodo dragon

There are some "dragons" that exist today. They don't breathe fire. They are not necessarily dangerous. One is the Komodo dragon. Another one is the Bearded dragon.

Bearded dragon

The Komodo Dragon

    The Komodo dragon is the largest, heaviest lizard in the world. It is also one of the most dangerous! It has a poisonous bite. Most lizards are harmless. Not this one!

    While they do not breathe fire, they should be <u>avoided</u>. Most Komodo dragons live in warm, dry places. Luckily, Komodo dragons can only be found on a few islands in Southeast Asia.

The Bearded Dragon

The Bearded dragon is different than a Komodo dragon. It is a small, gentle lizard. It makes a lovely pet. It likes human companionship and can become great friends.

Bearded dragons can grow to be several feet long. When they are young, they are just a few inches in length. They fit in the palm of your hand! They slowly increase in size.

Komodo dragons will eat animals as large as deer. They will attack other animals, too. Bearded dragons eat a much friendlier diet! They eat small insects, vegetables, and some fruits. They don't need to hunt for food if they are pets. They will be happy to let their owners feed them.

Are dragons real? Not in the way that fairy tales say. There are a few reptiles that take the name of dragon. One of them is very sweet. One of them is dangerous!

GLOSSARY

avoided
kept away from

companionship
a feeling of closeness and friendship

exist
to continue to be or live

sprints
runs at full speed over a short distance